# POEMS FOR THE NHS

## EDITED BY MATT BARNARD

Published by The Onslaught Press
19A Corso Street, Dundee, DD2 1DR
on 31 October 2018

ISBN: 978-1-912111-74-9

The poems are set in Le Monde Livre by Jean François Porchez.
The cover marries Juri Zaech's wonderful FRONTAGE
with Rae Kaiser's Birthday Doodles in the colours of the NHS

Printed & bound by Lightning Source

*An American Perspective*

*The NHS has lots of flaws,*
*the British people tell us,*
*but I'm not sympathetic 'cause*
*I'm busy being jealous.*

*Robert Schechter*

8    Foreword

11   Crisis Line—*Becky Balfourth*
12   Please Follow the Yellow Line—*Matt Barnard*
13   Mothers—*Diana Bell*
14   Head to Head—*Kaddy Benyon*
15   The Memory Clinic—*Roger Bloor*
16   On hearing for the first time—*Carole Bromley*
17   Changed—*Sarah J Bryson*
18   The Waiting Game—*Rachel Burns*
19   Chopin in the ICU—*David Canning*
20   Barium—*Mark Cassidy*
21   Chemo Nurse—*Keith Chandler*
22   Keeping Borzoi—*Claire Collison*
23   In Patient—*Clare Crossman*
24   Scapegoats—*Claire Crowther*
25   Mummy and the Night Sky—*Michelle Diaz*
26   Fracture—*Geri Dogmetchi*
27   Night operations—*Catherine Eunson*
28   The day you took my hand—*Sarah Evans*
29   Hospital Coffee—*Helen Fletcher*
30   Mrs Bate Addresses the College of Physicians, 1601—*Maggie Freeman*
32   it's about a man—*Wendy French*
33   Dear NHS—*Owen Gallagher*
34   on the slab—*Mark Gilbert*
35   Heartbeat—*Jenny Hammond*
36   Dancing with a Crab—*Alexander Hamilton*
38   Blood Letting—*Lucy Hamilton*
40   Haiku—*John Hawkhead*
41   When He Qualified—*Beda Higgins*
42   Unexpected Benefits of Phototherapy—*Angi Holden*
43   The Weight of Everything—*Amanda Huggins*
44   Coma—*Mimi Khalvati*
45   Psalm—*Joanne Limburg*
46   Nye's Ark—*Bernadette Lynch*
48   Visiting Time—*Julie Lumsden*
49   Student—*Roy Marshall*

50   Pronunciation Lessons in the Labour Ward—*Al Mcclimens*
51   The Surgery I go to Has a Two-headed Doctor—*Thomas McColl*
52   The Breast-Screening Unit—*Gill McEvoy*
53   Mitral valve replacement—*Sue MacIntyre*
54   Reflections of the Man in the Iron Mask—*Gordon Meade*
55   Visit—*Gillian Mellor*
56   In Our Hands—*Joan Michelson*
57   The countless times you've saved me, thankfully—*Kate Noakes*
58   Medicine—*Lucy Newlyn*
60   I Remember L.A.2—*Colin Newton*
62   In Defense of Typhus—*Nick Pallot*
64   On Muybridge Ward—*Matthew Paul*
65   Orthopaedic Surgeon—*Mel Pryor*
66   All these things that I have done—*Anna Rankin*
67   Radiography—*Angela Readman*
68   Crohn heroine—*Jude Rosen*
69   Birth Rite—*Carole Satyamurti*
70   Bath—*Myra Schneider*
71   On a narrow bed—*Finola Scott*
72   Love Song in a Bleached Room—*Kathryn Simmonds*
74   On the ceiling—*Penelope Shuttle*
75   Poem for Badger—*Reuben Roy Smith*
76   The State Of The Asylum—*Ruth Steadman*
77   Picket Line, April 2016—*Hannah Stone*
78   In the waiting room—*Alan John Stubbs*
79   Night Before an Operation—*Grant Tarbard*
80   Ultrasound—*Ali Thurm*
81   Topical Iodine—*Angela Topping*
82   Inside-out—*Susannah Violette*
84   Long-Term Prognosis—*Ruth Valentine*
85   Legacy—*Fiona Ritchie Walker*
86   A Medical History—*Richard Westcott*
88   Guy's Hospital, October 2015—*Natalie Whittaker*
89   Endoscopy—*Joe Williams*
90   For Mary, Ward 26—*Sue Wood*

92   **Notes & Acknowledgements**
98   **Biographies**

# Foreword

The idea for this anthology came out of personal experience. My two children were born through the NHS, I've made numerous visits to A&E and had surgery five or six times (mostly as the result of sports injuries or my own carelessness). All of those experiences have had a significant effect me, some of which have made their way into poems. Looking through the submissions to the anthology, the vast majority of poets shared with me the fact that their poems came out of personal experiences, often deeply personal.

There are poems here about receiving life-saving treatment, about the people who deliver that treatment with empathy and resilience, about friends and family and their intimate journeys and about the impact of both ill-health and of the interventions aimed at curing it or alleviating its effects. It is also, inevitably, a book about bodies. There is nothing like illness to remind us that we are defiantly not brains in jars, but corporeal beings with arms and legs, penis's and breasts, and that all that flesh is part of who we are. That we don't just live in our bodies but through our bodies.

We generally use the NHS when we or our loved ones are at our most vulnerable, and therefore the care the NHS gives us is at our time of greatest need. Yet, while we rightly celebrate it, it is important to remember that what makes the NHS great can also be a weakness. It is almost inevitable that such a huge institution that receives an enormous amount of public funding, will develop its own culture, language, and ways of working. These can baffle the outsider, and at its worst, the NHS is a place that forgets the importance of the individuals within it and sometimes closes ranks against them. Poetry is an art form that is especially suited to subtlety and nuance, and some of the poems in the anthology grapple with these complex issues.

But the overriding spirit of the anthology is one of celebration. The fact that the NHS is free at the point of use means we don't have to worry about a doctor's or a hospitals bill, for which we must be profoundly grateful. Our NHS is the envy of many around the world, and you just need to look at countries without an NHS to appreciate the potentially devastating result of a system where your ability to access medical care depends on the lottery of good or bad fortune.

I would like to thank all the poets who have contributed to the anthology and also all those who submitted poems but that we weren't able to include. Every one had an important story to tell. I would also like to thank Mathew Staunton and all those at The Onslaught Press who made this anthology possible. We hope it is a fitting way to mark 70 years of an extraordinary institution.

*Matt Barnard*
*Editor*

# Crisis Line

I'm tired-to-wired. My mind is a beast,
burning to eat itself. From down the line,
the voice is a quiet palm, raised in the air.
She doesn't say *calm down*, that old red flag.
Nor *take a bath, a walk, a cup of tea*.
My thoughts are teeth and claws.
They tear, they gouge, they rip, they do not
drink tea. My torn throat bears witness.
She hears this, and listens.

My words skitter into the silence.
They are jumpy. I don't trust them.
But in my fear, I try to trust her quiet.
My mind is wearing itself out, roaring
into the calm. Its claws, its teeth, its tongue
begin to slow. It drinks the listening like water.
As it breathes and breathes again, the world seems safer.

*Becky Balfourth*

# Please Follow the Yellow Line

The old are here, cluttering up corridors
that have no windows and that lead to rooms
which also have no windows. The old and infirm.

We are a motley crowd, we have missing teeth
and excess weight. Some of us hear
through fathoms of water. Sometimes we fail

to understand what is expected of us
and we think it matters. It feels like it matters.
There is a code that is spoken slowly.

The woman at reception tries to explain
and we all listen in expectantly, just in case.
I think you need Lung Function. Lung Function.

*Matt Barnard*

# Mothers

*Written on the Children's Cancer Ward*

We wait in corners
a moment, an hour.
There is the soft sound
of slippers on shiny surfaces.
Light bounces
from white walls.
The air is dry
and our mouths are dry
with the fear of loss.
Joy is the gentle
touch of fingertips
on skin.
A distant hum
descends on our shoulders
and shadows outside
grow longer.
Nothing is said,
but between us we build
a new understanding
in silence.

*Diana Bell*

# Head to Head

*(for Kate—after visiting Ward A3)*

Kate had brain surgery yesterday.
Glancing down at her phone to Google

the title of a book she can't remember,
I see the V-shaped dressing stuck

to the top of her stubble head,
beneath it, a spill of dried iodine:

new island arising on an atlas.
She introduces me to her nurse,

Arsad from the Philippines,
who checks her oxygenation levels,

temperature, blood, and I watch
as he serenely peels layers of white

tape from her wrist to remove her
from a three-tapped cannula.

They lean in like that, tête-à-tête,
as if unpuzzling something together

and I think: *How tenderly he holds her
hand in his in order to set her free.*

Afterwards, she packs her bag—slowly,
slowly—eats a little fruit salad, chats

until Arsad comes back to give her
the discharge letter, pain relief, a hug.

*Kaddy Benyon*

# The Memory Clinic

Set apart and distanced
by a woolly hat in a warm room
passive and perplexed he waits
with 'why and when'
nipping at his worried heel.
Then Doreen, hand placed gently on his knee
calm and caring from her bag produces
flask and sandwiches
and in that brief distracted rest
from 'why and when' the two hold hands
and picnic in the past.

*Roger Bloor*

# On hearing for the first time

'It sounds very very high'

and she sobs for the joy of it,
for the reds and blues of it,
the shock, the hullabaloo,

the kerfuffle, the Sturm und Drang,
the sudden ice cream in a shake,
the sherbet firework burst.

'It's just amazing' she cries
her face in her hands.
'I'm going to say the months of the year'

and she hears them, shaking,
'January February March'
April overwhelms her.

It's like never having seen a bird,
or the sea or the stars
never tasting an orange,

like living all your life in a cave
and coming out into the light,
the sun on your face.

Afterwards she walks by the Tyne,
daren't go alone for fear
the birdsong, the traffic, the ship's hooter

will be too much. They are not.
It's like falling in love.

*Carole Bromley*

# Changed

Behind the yellow lit hospital
the daylight leaches from the sky.
Inside she'll see her father

with a morphine pump,
a stark sheet against his skin, and overhead,
an anglepoise lamp turned to the wall

and she'll wait, with the others,
watching his respiration stumble to a halt
knowing how everything

will be changed after he's gone.

After he's gone, she stands to leave
and at the door looks back.
He lies alone on an island of reflected light.

She wades across the gulf to reach him
to lean down and kiss
his five o'clock-shadowed, unresponsive cheek.

Then she goes. He would not want a fuss.

*Sarah J Bryson*

# The Waiting Game

My grandfather haunts me,
as I sit in the waiting room.
I see his face in all the old men
waiting their turn
coughing, wheezing the coal dust
from their knackered lungs.
I smile in acknowledgement
at the breathless man beside me
he nods back from under his flat cap
the nurse calls out my name.
*Lie back and relax*, the nurse injects
nuclear venom into my veins.
*Will they glow in the dark?*
*My bones.*
*My bones.*

Afterwards, I'm herded back
to the waiting room, *sit and wait,*
*the nurse will call you for the bone scan.*
I sit next to the old man.
He gives a sympathetic nod,
I look at my watch again.
My grandfather didn't set much store
in hospitals and tests.
*Ah din't trust them quacks*
*as far as ah can throw em.*
I just want it to be over.
I want to go home,
forget I'm not well.
The nurse calls my name
the old man adjusts his cap.
*Take care pet.*
*Take care pet.*

*Rachel Burns*

# Chopin in the ICU

Chopin is playing his Raindrop Prelude, eight drops per bar

**keep time with my drip;**

when I was asked to count backwards from ten

**I reached only eight**

before being sustained in a dreamless nocturne.

**I awake to the metronome,**

my heartbeat counting, strung intravenously to his piano,

across its octaves I feel the pulse of his fingers, their cadence,

**the liquid flow of melody,**

I hold my breath almost to the point of asphyxia

**over each tortured phrase,**

he asks me to give a number to describe my pain—eight,

it is always eight—so he summons the angels of morphine,

**their movements soft,**

their robes rustling like rain and gently they pedal my tongue,

*pianissimo,*

with eight drops fill my head with sweetness.

*David Canning*

# Barium

Unmelting, ambivalent companion:
your radiopacity probes our shortcomings;
can explain speech loss,
may also—heavy hearted—
delineate an apple core of cancer.

Not for firework green or luminous pigment,
nor as the taste of Harrogate water,
but in alimentary suspension—
that is how you are recalled:
the white pawn of diagnosis.

*Mark Cassidy*

# Chemo Nurse

How wonderful you are, bursting late
into this waiting room of politeness and fear
with its Hello/Country Life fantazines,
discreet fliers ('How to Stay Positive'),
help groups, homeopathic diets
and Chapel "just along the corridor"

without apology showing everyone
with a 'TA-DA!' whisk of your ocelot
the ladder running up your inside thigh
announcing without tact or holdback
in a half Brummie half Jamaican accent
how lucky it was you wore knickers today,

taking by the hand one by one
the women in not quite convincing wigs
or bald as an egg or surreal woollen hats
towards what you call your 'milking parlour',
talking 19 to the dozen so they hardly notice
being rigged up to the poison drips,

talking 19 to the dozen about the daughter
you left (late again) at her first school,
managing even among the moon-faced
and eyebrowless to raise a smile,
fitting the needle so they hardly notice
how difficult it is now to find a vein.

In this palace of fake cheerfulness
with its wipe clean smiles and flower prints
and a chaplain who asks if there is anything
all morning I hear naughty laughter
billowing out from behind the screens
and think: yes, you are The Real Thing.

*Keith Chandler*

# Keeping Borzoi

That was the summer you learned
there was a point to eyelashes,
and that having cancer didn't
make you nice—wasn't enough
of a thing in common. That the best

conversation was with a nurse, who
hadn't had lunch or much sleep
for a week, and sat with you
behind blue curtains
for the time it took

to draw your blood, while Magic FM
and an aviary of machinery
chirruped for her attention.
How, while wiping the soft
inside of your arm with something

cold, she told you she once did a runner
from a wine bar on the Isle of Wight,
kept Borzoi; how her boyfriend
worked at Wetherspoons
and hated it.

*Claire Collison*

# In Patient

In the afternoon I lie on my back
to listen to the voices in the ward.
They seem to sparkle in the light
caught on waters' surface, continuing
beyond the place where they have
fallen from the sun.

On the 9th floor propped on the hospital bed,
above the long white corridors,
they take me out to where the tide
exists, beyond the coffee rooms, trolleys,
porters, clinics and the heli pads
to where I can float again.

Wordless I am held up; much  as by
the earth,  salt water or a mild day
of autumn air  that is made of footsteps,
laughter and  faces  looking in.

The reach of hands seems a river,
and the rush of it lifts me above
the floors below, on a clear tunnel
of a rising, lighthouse beam.

*Clare Crossman*

# Scapegoats

In Cardio, for Lung Function,
under a pole suspending drugs,
a prison guard sits down, chained
to a bird in front.

The prisoner, wearing one of those
thin gowns that gape, stares at the wall's
promulgation: *Due to snow,
we're spreading grit today.*

The guard puts out her hand. She can't
reach magazines to read. She rests
and their bracelets shine.

*Claire Crowther*

# Mummy and the Night Sky

Those aren't stars love,
they are constellations of diseases

look, there's polio
caused by unwashed strawberries

and over there
the one that looks like a bear
that's diabetes

the big one is cancer—
you'll be more prone

if you bring daisies into the house
or wear a balaclava on Tuesday.

*Michelle Diaz*

# Fracture

I'm the wreck of a body that cried
wolf at the bottom of the stairwell.

They searched for me in the dark
while my breasts were playing games

of Sardines in the wardrobe.
Amongst woollen dresses hung

on silk hangers they found my belly
warm as a newborn lamb in a nest

of straw. Shelved cardigans succoured
my elbows. I was spilled everywhere,

my head in the bathroom sink, my liver
in the unmade bed, on the landing

in the cage of my ribs, a sparrow
beating its wings.  In the oven,

where the one who never cooks hides
the paperwork, my Last Will and Testament.

*Geri Dogmetchi*

# Night operations

My son's body is heavier, and now we're in a huddle, almost
standing on the dark sand, so near is the runway to the sea.
He's my drowsing little cub, and through the sort of savage
black that can run all day in those unpeopled forests
comes a weak and persistent droning. It is an approaching
plane, and it's coming in to land. Soon we're lit up
with juddering lamps for the quick delivery, a kind
of backwards birth, mother and boy climbing
into the plane with the nurse. This makes it well
after one before they cut through his gut in Glasgow—
and then the hospital daylight, after doctors wake him,
sees plastic warriors vanquishing beasts on his bed.
None of us, alone, can cope with what we're up against,
or see past the rattling flight, into the roar of the night.

*Catherine Eunson*

# The day you took my hand

Lying prone, inhaling
iodine, mind made
muzzy by pre-med,
eyelids forced open,

head cushioned firmly
into place. *Please try not
to move.* Eyes black-hole
wide, gazing into bright

blinding from
the coming scalpel cut,
removing clouds
of dimming vision.

Someone took my hand,
warm contact
skin on skin,
a thumb-stroke across

my palm, a calming
touch along
blue worm veins,
sheltering me from

the storms of fear,
steering me safely through
the black-night present,
until I reach the light.

*Sarah Evans*

# Hospital Coffee

Sometimes doctors come into the cafe bloody.
We're told not to serve surgeons if they're still in scrubs, but I serve them;
the doctors are so busy, they need to be kept going.

You can hear the herpetologist a long way off:
he sings and swears and talks to himself loudly—
it could be blustering shyness.
I get his large Americano ready,
he always acts surprised to see it waiting for him,
he forgets his stamp card so we card so we keep one behind the till,
he buys coffees for his students sometimes.

The machine screams into the milk.
He has blood on his shoe-covers.

'Ah, nectar!' he says, leaving.
I want to ask him how the liver purifies everything that goes into a man
and how he fixes it
but he needs a break.

I used to read Scripture and there is a chaplaincy here.
But the services never fit my shifts and it's for patients really.

*Helen Fletcher*

# Mrs Bate Addresses the College of Physicians, 1601

There he lay, my lords, in his cot in the kitchen,
and I drew the curtains around him when anyone came in
so they'd not see my fine strong husband withered
and yellow. 'Where's Father?' our sons said,
and I'd reply, 'He's working at St Paul's.'
'What's that groaning?' our daughters said,
and I'd say, 'This house is haunted, I'm sure.'

But on my own I held him
and he was baby-light in my arms
and I loved him as on the night we first coupled
under the great oak at the river side; and I carried him there
my lips on his hot cheek, in his hair. 'Listen,'
I said, 'to the sweet sound of the water,'
and he cried, 'Am I come to the bank of the Styx?'
and weighted me with despair.

I passed the Royal Exchange, honoured sirs.
Widow Austen was packing away all her phials and potions.
'Mistress Bate,' she said, 'why are you so laden?'
She drew back the sheet and gazed
at his gaping mouth, his drawn face.
'I thought I could cure him with love,' I said.

She rummaged for a ruby bottle.
'This syrup has cured princes of fevers and dukes of the pox.
Your husband's but a common man, a little will heal him.'
'I have no money,' I said.
'I'll give it you for your kitchen things,
your pots and pans, any tin dishes you may have.'

So I laid my husband in his cot, sirs,
and filled her shawl with every pan I had.
Then off she ran, rattling like a tinker.
The ruby bottle stood on the table.
I lit a single candle
and tipped the bottle to his lips.
Precious, precious, I thought, you'll make him live.

He swallowed, coughed and died.
Honoured sirs, why I'm here is this:
will you make the Widow Austen give me back
my pots and pans and my tin dish
so I and my family can live?

*Maggie Freeman*

# it's about a man

it's about a man who healed the sick
as far as he was able
and this is the man who begged for penicillin
to cure a child
as far as he was able
it's about a man who burnt Fleming's letter
when the answer came back, None to Spare
and it's about a man who spoke at the funeral
as far as he was able
and this is the man who seven decades later
still remembers the date on the letter he wrote
it's about a man who waits in his chair
for a nurse to bring him whisky and water
this is the man who drinks the New Year in
although it's a man who can no longer hear
who peers out of his frame
as far as he is able
who thinks his own thoughts
it's about a man who comforted others
death is inevitable, comes to us all
it's about a man who is showered daily
and who now understands
as far as he is able

*Wendy French*

# Dear NHS

I want all my bodily organs snipped,
placed on ice, then strapped to a moped,
rushed to a helicopter pad and dropped
to their new owners in Falcarragh, Tijuana
and Havana and my blood syphoned into ailing poets.

My heart, liver and eyes are to be forwarded
to a lyric tenor, a revolutionary peasant,
a salsa instructor. Once they are plumbed in
and the settling-in period is done, a weekend
of toasting will commence with potteen, tequila, and rum.

What's left on the operating table
I bequeath to the skin and limb graft unit,
the hair transplant centre and to the surgeons
who'll assemble with scalpels to peer and gasp
at my lower half, marvel at the god I must have been.

*Owen Gallagher*

# on the slab

ambulance queue
the light at the end
of the tunnel

crashing through swing doors
on the slab
feet first

obsidian window
Pluto and Charon
are watching and waiting

everyone sleeps
on crisp folded sheets
occasional bleep

wide awake
in the green grey darkness . . .
someone else's blood

visiting time
we all have latin names
also

the usual smalltalk
clouds gather
on the horizon

an old man turns the corner
the bag of plasma
swings from side to side

these walls this ceiling
I used to be afraid
of the needle

the sun rises
a rainbow
on his get-well card

*Mark Gilbert*

# Heartbeat

'And who can live,' said Mrs Midas
'with a heart of gold?' although
a heart constructed of baser metals
is helping to keep me alive.

I'd be content with an ordinary heart
if less rusted, busted and broken
its wires entangled like a ball
of thread that even the cat has forsaken.

I read that a patient's passion for football
began on the day she received the heart
of a footballer. If you need evidence
see how I live with a shiny machine,

how I've fallen in love with glittery things
like a jackdaw, all things that twinkle
and flicker and gleam, that glint and glisten
glow with a sheen and lift my spirits.

Look up on high when the weather is right
at the night sky all spangled with light.
Look down now on the frosted ground
at star-struck dew in the morning brightness.

See the play of light on water in motion
through the spin of a breeze near a bridge
or even a puddle collecting reflections
of sunshine, like gold of a King long dead.

*Jenny Hammond*

# Dancing with a Crab

There is no 'excuse me' when dancing with the Crab.
Being a wallflower is not an option. You won't know he's there
until he sidles up and says, 'Are you dancing?'
No good saying 'Are you asking?'
This is an invitation you can't refuse.
Taking your hand, he leads you out of your life.
This is a dance without a tune, which is strange,
with it's 'Slow, slow, quick, quick slow' start.
First, he lurks deep in the dark innermost place,
confidant he will not be found, silly Crab.
There are ways of seeking him out.
Your partner is looked for, where is the Crab hiding?
Are its pincers well attached? Will it come quietly?
Or will it need a scalpels nudge?   A scan, so like a crab pot,
catches and reveals its whereabouts. Your Crab is invited to leave the dance.
But your partner likes the dark. 'A bowel? Been here, twice,'
And indeed, he has, and each time was caught and cut.
Now your Crab has gone travelling, 'Mmh, a lung, how nice
and pleasantly air conditioned, this will do.'
But the Crab Catcher is not deceived, and casts its scan
your Crab is found again. The Catcher is confidant
chooses to poison the Crab and pursues it with chemicals.
And begins to unseat the Crab, to reduce its grip,
no longer a menace now just a nuisance.
But the Crab is wily, and waits and waits.
He creeps ever so slowly, no noise, not a bang nor a rattle
but the Crab Catcher is also wily, another scan finds the Crab
having beaten off the chemo attack, he is quietly growing again.
But the Catcher is aware of such a move, and plans to catch the Crab again.
And there he is again, tumouring nicely on the liver,
this time there is no hiding place, foolishly at large and found.

A device is inserted, a lethal spike that cooks the tumour inside out.
And where there was vibrant disease there is devastation, a charred ruin.
And now some new front opens, the lung is now the centre of attention,
And that too is attacked by surgical skill; the crab infested part is removed.
All we have to do now is wait to see if the dance has ended.
I don't hear the tune anymore,
but the band is still in the ballroom.
Waiting for an encore.
I have no intention of obliging.
But against my will there is a hint of music.

*Alexander Hamilton*

# Blood Letting

## I

The Engineer says the priest came to hear her confession but she couldn't think of anything terrible she'd done. [The dialyzer is the key to haemodialysis.] She is tearful & apologetic. Calls herself *grouchy mess* & *hysterical witch*. She's so wired-up that the 'ports' look like multi-coloured hair bobbins. [The average person has 10 to 12 pints of blood; during dialysis only one pint (about two cups) is outside the body at a time.] I collect up phone, cards & photo of L. Follow her bed out of the HDU back to the ICU. Sometimes her large brown eyes seem to rest on me.

## II

Sometimes her brown eyes settle on me. Like a butterfly on my skin. Her hair is feather-soft. She complains it hasn't been washed. [There are two sections in the dialyzer; the section for dialysate and the section for blood.] The nutritionist asks what she likes to eat. *Anything Mediterranean.* Then removes the untouched sausage & mash. [The two sections are divided by a semi-permeable membrane so they don't mix together.] I hold the Engineer's hand. We look at the photo of L. Fifteen & sitting her mocks.

## III

Other times her eyes are eloquent. Large white rather than brimstone yellow. The nurse explains why she keeps being moved between IC & HD. Her washed hair fans out dark against the pillow. [The dialysis solution is then flushed down the drain along with the waste.] We talk about medieval blood letting—she almost laughs. Doctors optimistic but. Stress situation might change & suddenly.

IV

Nor butterfly nor Engineer. Eyes barely slits in setae. No more to flit from iPhone to photo. Never to rest on me. Nor blood nor dialysate—the machines are silent, pushed aside. Her head seems slighter, hair curtained against her face, lips a little parted. One cold hand grips an olive wood cross. As I lean to kiss her brow, it's as if she chose to speak . . . *For, if I imp my wing on thine, affliction shall advance the flight in me.*

Lucy Hamilton

# Haiku

after the last dose
of radiotherapy
her feet remain cold


chemotherapy
we open the bottle of red
we had been saving


fading reminder
of that hard winter's moon
the scar on her breast


spring moon
I explore the lustrous trail
of her breast scars


*John Hawkhead*

# When He Qualified

He learnt to juggle hours,
to listen to ghosts, hear confessions,
to pick out nits and sew with dreams.

To patch a memory knit with notions,
to be a mouse, creep in cracks,
to forage and eat shades of grey.

To be wide-eyed day and night
to beetle hard-shelled, to learn
to love the comfort of cold walls.

To be another face in a sea of faces,
to forget what day his birthday is.
To be godless but yearn to pray.

*Beda Higgins*

# Unexpected Benefits of Phototherapy

The irony amuses her. All those years of slip, slap, slop,
of keeping the children protected from the midday sun,
of sunscreen no weaker than factor thirty-five,
of casting distain on the clients of Anita's Bronzing Parlour.
And now, here she is, sun-bedding, courtesy of the NHS.
The specialist (all varieties of eczema and psoriasis)
has examined her swollen skin, itchy and bleeding,
and declared her a suitable candidate for phototherapy.
She has asked about the patches high on her thighs,
made worse where the seams of her jeans chafe,
and the raw bands etched beneath her heavy breasts.
Expose them to the light, she's told. So three times a week,
here she stands, stripped to the wedding ring she still wears
even though he left months ago, slowly gyrating
to the theme tune of Tales of the Unexpected as it plays
through her head, wondering what he'd have made
of her 360 tan, her silky back, her golden Mound of Venus.

*Angi Holden*

# The Weight of Everything

The nurse, one hand pressed against her forehead
and the other against the wall,
looked up when she heard my footsteps pass,
smiled briefly, smoothed down her skirt
and turned back to the ward.

Later, at home, when I lay between cool sheets,
I closed my eyes and conjured her face,
understood the weight of everything her smile contained,
wondered if she was still watching over you
in the toss and turn of your hospital bed.

At dawn, I drove past quiet houses, dark, still filled with sleep,
stopped abruptly at a red light even though I was alone.
And as I waited I glimpsed a single bright lamp
in an upstairs room,
and wanted it to be her, safely home from her shift.

*Amanda Huggins*

# Coma

Mr Khalvati? Larger than life he was;
too large to die so they wired him up on a bed.
Small as a soul he is on the mountain ledge.

Lids gone thin as a babe's. If it's mist he sees
it's no mist he knows by name. Can you hear me,
Mr Khalvati? Larger than life he was

and the death he dies large as the hands that once
drowned mine and the salt of his laugh in the wave.
Small as a soul he is on the mountain ledge.

Can you squeeze my hand? (Ach! Where are the hands
I held in mine to pull me back to the baize?)
Mr Khalvati? Larger than life he was

with these outstretched hands that squeezing squeeze
thin air. Wired he is, tired he is and there,
small as a soul he is on the mountain ledge.

No nudging him out of the nest. No one to help him
fall or fly, there's no coming back to the baize.
Mr Khalvati? Larger than life he was.
Small as a soul he is on the mountain ledge.

*Mimi Khalvati*

# Psalm

O Night and Silence,
        why should I complain?

For though I am empty, and pale as veal,
        surely your servants are good.

I came here bloody, and they undressed me;
they cast aside my clothes,
        for they were soiled.

Into my veins
they pushed their merciful darkness.
Like a branch of its blossoms,
        they scraped me clean.

All night, they have watched over me;
they have lifted the sheets
        and marked my loss.

They tell me my loss is normal:
        yea, I am filled with statistics.

Hour by hour, their kindness drips;
        water and salt, the smaller mercies.

O Great Indifference,
        to whom should I complain?

*Joanne Limburg*

# Nye's Ark

*'It will provide you with all medical, dental and nursing care.
Everyone—rich or poor, man, woman, or child—can use it or any part of it'.*

NHS Information Leaflet, February 1948

Bring aboard the infirmaries and the cottage hospitals.
Let the old workhouses embark. Love them, tart them up,
give them friends. Build new ones that look like
the Starship Enterprise or a Rubik's Cube.
*Make yourself an ark of cypress wood.*

Find space for the stucco and redbrick, for concrete blocks,
for the plate-glass palaces with helipads; for the wards
named after the Duchess of York and the Rotary Club;
for the multi-faith centres and the morgues.
*Make rooms in it and coat it with pitch inside and out.*

Pack the vancomycin and the bandages. We'll need
crutches to support us, myrrh and morphine for the pain.
Don't forget the aloe vera and the echocardiograms.
Travel nowhere without IV drips and drains.
*The floodgates of heaven were opened.*

Bring on the chaplains and almoners, porters and chefs
and the Filipina nurse who misses her children.
Load up the volunteers and visitors, the surgeons
and the families who keep vigil in the night.
*I have found you righteous in this generation.*

There's a place for the nineteen-year-old from Mandeville
who comforts the ruminators; for the stalking nun
who swings her rosary beads; for the girl from the
Magdalene Laundries who polishes the parquet.
*The ark came to rest on the mountains of Ararat.*

Don't forget the neonate no big than a tenner,
nor the nonagenarian who danced again, nor the girl
from Maharashtra who got a new hip and mojo.
Lead by the hand those who struggle in their minds.
*Keep their various kinds alive throughout the earth.*

Welcome Eileen and Les and Pushpa and Precious,
Merlinda, Moreblessings, Susheela and Sue.
Bring on Doctor Cecera and Sister Delaney,
helpful Elsie, Kian and baby Lily-Mai.
*Be fruitful and increase in number and fill the earth.*

*Bernadette Lynch*

# Visiting Time

Briefly raising myself out of somnolence
in this pristine bed
to thank you, wordlessly, for bringing stuff—

although I prefer faux flowers—unchanging
colour and shape
season after season and never die on you.

Also annoyed when you described the winter trees
as dead. No. They sleep. Safely withdrawn.
See you in Spring.

*Julie Lumsden*

# Student

The first of my many dead; she washes, I dry,
dab his cheeks and lids, change the water, roll him,
rub a sheet crease from his back,
pat soft white buttocks, take out
catheter and cannula,
tape and press where blood pools,
thick as blackberry jam.

Julie's brisk, careful as a cook, talks to him
as if he could hear,  and there's something in me
of the little boy, aproned,  allowed to help;
his doughy-ness perhaps, or the talc like flour,
as if this privilege were a treat,
the finished parcel of taped sheets
something to be proud of.

*Roy Marshall*

# Pronunciation Lessons in the Labour Ward

Another D.O.A. to clerk. *The G*
*Is soft*, she tells them, *like geranium.*
The sister knows the routine. A teen mum
still shocked from a stillbirth. It's too easy
to get blasé. The midwife comes to see
how she's coping with the post-partum
haemorrhage before checking magnesium
in bloods and then she's got a D&C.

And baby George? Mum has the Polaroid
the nurses took. It's all she has. He's dead
and buried in her mind. People avoid
her gaze. She can't remember what was said
two minutes since. The G is hard. Her son,
like grief, like ghost, as good as gold, is gone.

*Al Mcclimens*

# The Surgery I go to Has a Two-headed Doctor
## (a.k.a. The government's latest cost-saving innovation for the NHS)

The surgery I go to has a two-headed doctor.
'Doctor Smith will see you, see you, now.'

It gets very confusing.
Doctor Smith, via his left head, gives me a diagnosis
then, via his right head, gives me a second opinion,
which always differs from the first
(and, as it happens,
that opinion's never the best one—
always the worst).

When Doctor Smith examines me with a stethoscope,
it's in the left head's left ear and the right head's right ear.
In other words, he makes a right pig's ear
(and also a left pig's ear) of any examination he does.
However, when I once challenged him about it,
Doctor Smith's left head simply said,
'Can you breathe in a bit more deeply, please?'
while his right head shook morosely.

Apparently, his wife has got two heads as well,
and two pairs of breasts.
It's said they met as impoverished
but physically normal students,
earning money by undergoing laboratory tests.

Two heads are better than one, they say,
but I'm not too sure that comes into play
while attending an appointment with
the always-in-two-minds Doctor Smith.

*Thomas McColl*

# The Breast-Screening Unit

We are women of that' certain age',
used to saying please and thank you
as if it were a privilege or a pleasure to be here,
having our breasts slammed and stretched between
the armoured plating of machines.

We're handed baskets like the ones
we'd use in supermarkets except
that these hold gowns and robes in pink.
Tactful staff escort us to the cubicles—
"Thank you very much" we say, bustling
into sardine cans to change.

We flutter out, pink angels in our robes,
settle on the chairs. The room blooms
like a vase of quiet roses.
Strange how we sit, so well-behaved,
waiting our turn for the filleting of flesh.

*Gill McEvoy*

# Mitral valve replacement

The anteroom to white,
welcome into blank, the rosy nurse—

no quick goodbye.
The record of those hours—

a bright stamp on whiteness,
a scar, a fall like raspberry jam

between my breasts.
What did the surgeon say?

'Your heart was leaping
around—so hard to get hold of.'

How easy quick falling
into a void, how slow

needing all fibres
to come back again from

all that knife work, needlework,
theatre life I heard about.

*Sue MacIntyre*

# Reflections of the Man in the Iron Mask

From here, I am able to smell
the fear of the previous patients.
Or is it my own? We are all so alike
with our trousers down, and our faces
no more than a few inches away

from the black plastic cradles
on which we are prone. When
the switch is flicked, I can hear
the whirr of the machines as it repositions
itself to deliver its differing doses

of radiation. It will all be over,
if not in the blink of an eye, then
at least no longer than the time
it takes to make a decent espresso.
When I change back into my day

clothes, my forehead still retains
the impression of the mask, a red
rim painted in above my eyebrows,
and along the sides of my cheekbones.
I am somehow unable to see it

on the faces of the other patients.
I must press mine too firmly into
the mask, either wanting to lose myself
completely in it or, for it to become,
permanently, a part of myself.

*Gordon Meade*

# Visit

For my son's birthday
I am in hospital again.
This time he is not here.
Illness doesn't celebrate
special events.

He saw me yesterday
wired up to everything.
I told him I stayed in bed all day,
watched so much daytime tv—
a student again with little to study.

I showed him my TED stockings
whiter than the sun starved skin
on my freaky, swollen feet.
Tomorrow is the day
I have to sit in a chair.

It will take three nurses
to help me: one will move
the drain, one the catheter bag,
one will hold my arm
and move the drip.

The excitement will make me pass out.
I'll slump in my chair,
come round grinning
like a goon desperate to share my news—
I've taken my first steps.

*Gillian Mellor*

# In Our Hands

Your number isn't coming up,
nor any other, not the number
for the man beside you,
nor for the women beside him,
nor for the boy who's complaining
to his mum, who adds her voice,

not for any in the rows,
not for any in the room,
not for any in the wing,
nor parked along the corridor,
nor coming back in a min',
nor coming back tomorrow.

Free from the point of entry/delivery/use
—health care. But not today,
and not tomorrow, or tomorrow.
For long it was and it may be again,
but who knows how? Who knows when?
Now is not the time. Let's go. Goodbye.

*Joan Michelson*

# The countless times you've saved me, thankfully

When I turn into a weird land fish,
drowning in my own air, you skip me
to the head of the queue.

Nebulise fist. Questions later.

As the drugs start their gas magic
in my lungs, I can speak without gasping
like a round mouthed carp.

You ask what it was this time.

Perhaps the woman next to me
at Sunday lunch had been out riding.
Clue: she might've been wearing jodhpurs.

Breathe now. Breathe.

Maybe unwittingly I'd visited a new place
with invisible traces of cat.
Note to self: remember to enquire.

Breathe deeply now. Breathe.

I've not crossed the Sahara lately,
so put it down to any one of: pollen,
generally and everywhere,

house dust mites (faeces thereof),
grass cuttings, pollution.
There's enough of that these days.

Keep breathing now. Deeply. Breathe.

*Kate Noakes*

# Medicine

When I saw you lying there,
your oxygen-mask slipping,
you were not yourself, but your father—
dead on the Somme.
I was not myself, but a witness to World War One,
and another war impending.
There weren't enough nurses for the wounded and dying.
The trench was deep, the duck-boards strained
under thick-piled bodies.
Your death-to-come was a tiny pin-point
on a lengthening graph;
your father's name picked out among the un-numbered.
and I, with my survivor's guilt, remained by your side
the whole night through to watch it happening.
Then I became a prophet-healer,
chosen as the Special One to save the world—
and I was shouting, shouting.
Then I was imprisoned in a ward,
watched by an eye in the door, to stop me escaping.
When I had slept, they let me out to see you.
My kind gaoler, Norah, came with me
to read from The Guardian,
let you know what was happening.
Later, they let me see you alone.
Morning after morning I sat beside you
in your lonely ward.
The nurse squeezed your hand;
a Jamaican said 'bless', with a voice
that rose and fell like music.
I read you poems—the ones I loved.
I was sure, once and once only, that you heard me.
Whose death was I mourning, before and after?

Whose story is this anyway—
Yours, or your generation's passed down to me?
Day after day, outside your window,
a blackbird sang in the tree.

*Lucy Newlyn*

"Keep very still!"

Young women lean over my prone body,
deftly manoeuvring me into the desired position,
on achieving which I must
    keep very still.

I wish that laser beam were a bit further from my eyes.
Just shift a fraction to get the line-up right,
and then again
    keep very still.

I wiggle my toes defiantly inside my shoes.
I'm a bit of a rebel, you see;
but my head I
    keep very still.

"This is where things get a bit dangerous,
so we'll nip outside while you endure the radiation.
See you
    keep very still."

Mechanisms whirr and click, photon torpedoes lock on.
I count the seconds while the rays pour into me,
though not on my fingers, which
    keep very still.

Rays of death are working to prolong my life,
excising cancer. Should it not work,
I'll have no choice but to
    keep very still.

That's all for today.  But may I have my glasses back?
I don't want to walk into a wall, although
having fallen, I might
      keep very still.

I check the latest changes to my appointments.
Why are the times forever being switched around?
Why don't they have to
      keep very still.

I collect my coat from the waiting room.
The speaker on the wall plays Radio Therapy.
The next patient prepares to
      keep very still.

*Colin Newton*

# In Defense of Typhus

I would reappraise the tapeworm, stowaway in the gut's hold, vicarious
forager of others' nutrition, genius of the extempore, uninvited to life's feast,
blind phantom invisible in the intestines' labyrinthine sewer.
I would reassess the mosquito, blood-addict, every gram a mythical beast,
seeker of heat and the haemoglobin needed to lay, fearless angel of death,
ignorant of her lethal wake, quintessence of altruism, long deceased

before her transmissions go viral, before the larvae she'll never know hatch.
I would reconsider these prodigies of survival, these unthinking dependants
    who cling
to us though we would exterminate them, we who would humour a squirrel,
startled deep in a waste-bin, its childish mischief, its panic, its noxious
    re-scattering,
we who could watch a chick snatched by a pike, aghast how close had lurked
the tiger to the lamb, distraught for the moorhen, a Ceres mourning her
offspring,

yet who would thrill too at this eruption of darkness, this collision of
    elements.
So let neither scale nor contagion belie even your innocence, my little mite,
oblivious as a courtesan of how the imprint of your passion festered,
how infected I became, through our one-night stand, through your love-bite,
how delirious with time-travel, with virtual tableaux of gaol-yards and
    tenements,
with whirligigs of dust and pus, my guileless parasite.

Night was a prison-hulk where you chilled to a shroud sheets
drenched in sweat, day a ghetto scorched by the spores of your toxic lips.
From ice-age to catastrophic climate-change your fever pitched me.
In an hour I shivered with the mammoth, burned in a man-made apocalypse.
But you never heard plague-pits opening, their dead stirring against you,
never foresaw, in your simplicity, how genius incubates its own eclipse.

I felt you dissolve in the medicinal cool of dawn, in the daybreak of those
  ghosts.
Too late, I greet you as intimate, as vector of inflammatory truth, as my
  analogy.
I would deliberate with you which of us carries the more virulent germ,
which of us, parasite or man, in fuller consciousness yet of less necessity,
overheats an involuntary host. I would re-examine mosquito and tapeworm.
Must vision be so diminished, now we have microscopes to see?


*Nick Pallot*

# On Muybridge Ward

As ever, Dad has his eyelids clamped shut.
I've never seen him so stubbly and rough.
'Would you like a shave, Michael?' asks Millie,
the auxiliary. He opens one eye
and closes it. She takes that as a yes,
or not a no anyway; assembles,
in a jiffy, all the requisite kit.
Millie and I behold an ample squirt
of shaving-foam ballooning on her palm.
'It's like a yummy great spoonful of cream,'
says Millie. We chuckle. Gently, with grace,
she lathers Dad into Father Christmas.
He flinches as if it's murder. She chides
him, 'A handsome man like you, Michael, needs
to look his best with us lovely people
around you.' She dips the disposable
razor in a bowl of tepid water.
Her tongue-tip protrudes from the corner
of her mouth. She reminds herself to go
with the grain. Dad's calm, unfurrowed brow
brings a bodhisattva look to his face.
Millie works with a zeal becoming haste.
At the dimple I inherited, then
handed down, in turn, to my three children,
she brakes. 'This bit's so tricky—how on earth
do you manage it?' I'm not quite sure if
she's asking Dad or me. 'Pain in the butt,'
I mutter. Millie begins to towel-pat
his mustard-yellow cheeks. Dad resists: 'Clear off!
*Gertcha!*' Millie and I can't help but laugh.
'Well now, Michael, you look gorgeous!' she cries.
For the briefest time, Dad opens both eyes.

*Matthew Paul*

# Orthopaedic Surgeon

It was the way he strolled into that dun, welcome lounge
in a moss jumper like a liberal in combat trousers
with *the one* written all over his high, Renaissance face,
the way he took her eye with a medic's level appraisal
that stripped her zippered dress, her tights, her flesh,
the way he signed himself in with a biro flourish
as if writing his name on the rest of her night.
She was sure the crack in the paintwork mouth-height
behind him opened its lips a bit more, then more
when he smiled, extended his hand. Her heart's aorta
splintered. She thought she was an amputee.
She thought she was on amphetamines,
wanted to put her hooped ear like a stethoscope
to the left camber of his chest and the pulse below
while she stroked her flux and grip
into the arms, the legs, the impeccable fingers
she'd have squeezing the love out of her like bandages.

*Mel Pryor*

# All these things that I have done

You have danced and twirled under a midnight canopy
Choosing to bring in the dawn
But no all nighters next to a beeping monitor

You have cried for the lover who made you forget who you were
But you cocooned out,
magnificent
Whilst I emerged
wings shredded, matted in mulch
Grounded

You have painted on canvases
Leaving rainbow stains
But as yet have not drenched your hands in magenta clots

You laughed wildly at the paper masche sculptures of unidentifiable modern art
But not sombrely etched a name
on a stone

You wished time away frivolously
Whilst I held onto seconds
like the edge of a cliff

You have drowned aimlessly in another's eyes
Finding layers of life
You didn't know existed
Whilst I watched the hour glass slip through pupils

You thought you understood the importance of holding a hand
You don't
And you won't
Till their fingers go limp

*Anna Rankin*

# Radiography

He lifts the picture of her bones
to the light, holds it close to the bulb

to show me my mother full of leaves
in autumn, baring the steel

of their scaffolding to the wind.
And I want to hold him

for tickling streams with a stick,
cracks in the lake I've skated for years,

felt split under my feet. I didn't know
inside her would look so beautiful,

cool as spilled ink, a cyanotype of years,
those shadows in her head the shape

of a polar bear sniffing an evening,
nosing through the ice.

*Angela Readman*

# Crohn heroine

*The bed had a ramp, a 'sit up and take notice of you' bed with a plastic undersheet to catch any slip ups. The sheets were creased with brownish streaks—dried blood —they weren't for changing. The bed leaked fluids it didn't have. In the middle of the night I sat bolt upright and naked Are there mosquitoes here? I inquired. What do you think you're at the seaside? the nurse retorted.*

The itching went on all night and then at six everyone
woke up when I conked out. My bed floated in the sea, the pain
was on the end of a telephone line I could hear faintly
in the distance. The bed blew up into a lilo that floated
into the Mediterranean—middle earth between
the ephemeral and the divine—and I dived under water
exploring corals and angel fish. Seaweed garlanded
my arms, tangling with the telephone wires—I wasn't completely
cut off. I floated out of my body looking down
from the sea clouds on the husk with its dented metal casing
and crumpled mesh. Sparklers were shooting out, fizzing
and spurting. I heard inchoate shouting far away.
After *Give me high five*, I rejoined the lilo that blew up
into an airship and I was tripping on the bed in an air bubble.
At first it hit me as a vacuum—the sticky electricity
stopped crackling in my head and my blood tamed and then
I felt heat, real heat that claws black to ash, cools lava
to pumice stone, lolling froth and burning and I knew
there must be air though there was nothing to breathe
but hot froth, frothing magma surging up, retching up
from the earth's bowels, where mud settles, charcoal
sediments. It left fossils in the mould like crows' feet
in bark and whitened bone of emptied sockets.

*Jude Rosen*

# Birth Rite

Since I've not known another birth
this surgery seems natural.
I've left my home
and have come here
to be prepared.

You are my grail
and I must purify myself—
be stripped, shaved, emptied,
wrapped in white—
before I gain you.

Soon you'll be lifted
from the domain of wishes
and we who have been so intimate
will touch at last. Perhaps
we'll be awkward with each other.

Hiss of trolley wheels,
haze of lights . . . I'm drawn
through deepest passages,
protected, raised; someone
holds my hand perfectly.

To be reborn with you
I shed responsibility,
my social face,
speech, consciousness.
I reach back to the dark.

*Carole Satyamurti*

# Bath

Kindness, an Irish lilt in her voice,
spares me the effort of running the water
and supports my elbow when, stripped
of everything but wound dressings,
I take a giant step into the tub.

Warm water wells into my crotch,
unlocks spine, lullabies stomach.
Is it because I've passed through
extremity that this comfort is intense
as the yellow that daffodils trumpet?

Yesterday—my raw body stranded
by the basin, chill sprouting on my skin
while a Chinese student nurse
conscientiously dabbed each
helpless area—is miles away.

Dimly, I remember a stark room
and the high-sided saltwater bath
I was dipped in a few days
after giving birth. As Kindness
babies my back with a pink flannel

I'm reborn though maimed, ageing.
And this pool of bliss can no more
be explained than the song that pours
from a lark as it disappears into
stitchless blue, the seed circles

that cram a sunflower's calyx,
day splashing crimsons
and apricot golds across the sky
before it seeps into the silence
of night, the way love fountains.

*Myra Schneider*

# On a narrow bed

tubes anchor my outstretched hands
violent bruises marble my skin

not everywhere but deep in my core
blackness suckles me

my womb offers a Jack O'Lantern grin
its mouth smirks with metal teeth

displaced organs wander to find
new homes in hesitant spaces

pain panics beats my drum-tight wound
grasped shut by snarling staples

from the foot of the bed I hear
a white-coated lad ask
how are we today?

mute I struggle shift
position and break
wind

*Finola Scott*

# Love Song in a Bleached Room

I wait for a long time before Anya comes:
off-duty she smiles and my skin goes electric.
Take me home, I say through my unmoving mouth.

Aren't you asleep yet? She asks.
Not asleep, I say with my nearly dead lips.

There is a moon outside or no moon. The lawn
stripes with light or no light. In the pavement cracks
insects are living their unexamined lives.

Anya won't talk when she's tightening the tourniquet.
My veins are so fat I almost giggle—
swollen rivers to places I've forgotten existed.

She tells me not to think too hard,
it's bad for my readings. She charts me like a ship
despite the fact that I'm anchored safely to the bed.
If you try to jump there's fuss—

the lifejackets taste of bitter rubber,
the lighthouse comes straight for your eyes.

*Anya*, If I say her name forty, fifty times, it means
nothing, it's merely sound let loose.
My eyelashes are on the brink of extinction but

my arms still work. Up and down they go
when I ask them to. All right when I plead.

Anya knows my arms were not always like this.
I could sing once, I tell her with blinks,
show tunes and passages of light opera.

Her curls are shiny like ribbon
or frazzled with fatigue, and either way I wish
I could touch them.

*Kathryn Simmonds*

# On the ceiling

The dead are writing on the ceiling
but the surgeons don't look up,

the dead are writing
all sorts of interesting things

on the ceiling,
but dear dead people, why use invisible ink?

The dead are writing on the ceiling
as if their deaths depended on it,

if you squint up
maybe you'll see some of their words

flickering between this world
and the next,

the dead are writing about life and death,
but the cardiac teams won't look up,

they keep dragging the death away,
then the dead grab it back,

float up through the ceiling,
free at last

*Penelope Shuttle*

# Poem for Badger

1
You wanted to run away with me
You said for me to get your clothes
and visit the cash point
'Why do you need money?', I asked
'For the taxi to escape
we have drink and food at home'.
I tried to explain that you were
tubed up and had a catheter
on your willy.
You denied this and pleaded still for me to take you home,
I called for the support staff who confirmed
you couldn't leave your bed,
two weeks later
you were dead.

2
You died before the clocks
went forward
a necessary death as necessary
as my essential tremor.
I was on the phone to the evening nurse
when she asked me to hold on
and came back
rather too quickly
to tell me you had passed away.
'Tell them I am dead'
you had said.
Several friends have said hospitals sometimes know
of deaths to happen.
You died while I was on the phone and
you didn't die alone
we had a connection.

*Reuben Roy Smith*

# The State Of The Asylum

A magpie hawks his wares in the long damp yellow grass.
*Look up!* He struts in black and white; *the sky is falling
fast.* These keys feel so official I'm not sure I can trust them.
The building squats to pee under a low grey sun.

*We've seen refugees and anorexics, paedophiles and veterans,
smuggled aid to starving bishops, absolved the dying desperate.
We've recycled every tear that's stained the threadbare carpet.
Do come on in, dear—your pain is safe with us.*

Hope with her hoover and undertaker eyes: *Swim, people, swim!*
—like the recently bereaved. We count our peanuts in a line
(licking blood from our fingers), tune the radio for news,
board up the window's final view, sing as all the stars expire.

*A quaint and charming doer-upper with original features:
an ECT suite, a padded cell—for sale to the highest bidder.*

*Ruth Steadman*

# Picket Line, April 2016

It is strange to see them standing in a row
with hands holding only placards,
not lifting a swollen limb
or depressing a tongue with a wooden stick.

Scarves not stethoscopes hang round their necks;
woollen, not latex, gloves protect their hands.
No one asks them 'how long have you felt like this?'
or 'on a scale on one to ten how bad is your pain?'

They want a consultation with the man in charge,
they need him to come and sit
in the chair they've kept free
at the negotiating table.

It is cold today on the picket line;
flurries of snow ghost the new leaves,
the wind flaps at the scrubs they wear
bunched under thick coats.

There is no brazier. They give me a lapel badge.
All I have to offer is biscuits; they thank me and smile,
add them to the stockpile they will share
when their shift here is over, and they return to the wards.

*Hannah Stone*

# In the waiting room

ones with the proper paperwork who had
quietly answered all of the usual proof
of identities whispered across the desk
were now seated uncomfortably on a bendy
plastic chair catching at names released

to the air as a summons to one of the
strange

mouthy doors as a man nudges
his neighbour and slyly opens a cupped

hand to reveal

embedded deep—a thick nail
stake in meaty flesh that bleeds


*Alan John Stubbs*

# Night Before an Operation

Mentally, all my luggage was packed,
black bags deseed my packing-crate eyes

as I drank slowly the hours medicine,
the spider bite fed on my neck.

My pupils turned white without speech
as I burst into dust from clay and back again,

these raw materials that anticipate dissection,
a golem kneaded my shoulders.

In the night ward Vermeer's bulb
has burnt out its filament,

no longer is the evening painted
with burnished light, pitch swallowed

by a tattered jacket of black, of congealed ash
that sticks to the back of the throat.

I use Egyptian blue ink to paint my
eyes shut, and in my pyjama pocket folds

there're a hundred painted idols that keep guard
over my clay pudding until the next day.

*Grant Tarbard*

# Ultrasound

Pushing down on belly and uterus,
     the nurse prepares your horoscope,

measures each limb and heart valve
     draws lines from star to star.

Stinging scorpion, archer,
     capricious goat or water bearer—

pixellated star of the silver screen
     your constellation rises to meet me.

*Ali Thurm*

# Topical Iodine

Blue as school ink with rumours of purple,
medicinal perfume to scent our scrapes,
blossoming on skin, bestowed by crisp nurses.

A bleeding knee was dabbed with sapphire drops,
its sting soon forgiven, as Rorschach blots
spread their magic, dripped into white socks.

How many times I fell in the yard
to exchange dull assembly for a walk alone
through streets silent of school clatter, fizzing rhymes

forming themselves in my mouth, the copper of
rainy pavements leading to sky-blue railings,
stone steps, wedged-open clinic doors:

antiseptic spells, where there were no bullies,
no screaming teachers, but a hushed routine,
lace-ups squeaking on polished floors.

I tried words for size, like *tincture* and *chemical*,
words I was too young to spell, though their rhythms
chimed in my ear, saved up like cajoled coins.

My iodine days, those blue forgotten mornings,
now obsolete, half a century away from here,
scented like parma violets, sweet on my tongue.

*Angela Topping*

# Inside-out

the cotton of my dress

breathes in
breathes out

like a ventilator drifts on grey lino

the ward is
a held breath
a forgotten life

there is a nurse, of course there is
—eventually
(it is a Sunday)

I feel it as if she is already there

my veins
are on the outside
blooming flowers
each stab

blue as crushed berries
—it's all I can think of

drawn from inside out
at the corner of
my elbow

not the crook!
not the goddamn crook!
I am incredulous
enough to gasp

as if it were her, my nurse
tearfully I hug the circular plaster
my arm, myself

*Susannah Violette*

# Long-Term Prognosis

The doctors are saying that there's every chance
there will be a chance, that something new will happen,
you'll be feeling something you're not feeling today,
that morning will come and you'll be here to see it

or be here but not see it. The doctors are saying
they are doing their best. They're saying they understand
more than they don't understand, that your condition
is stable, given the trembling of the stars

and the circulation of breath. All the good doctors
are wringing their hands or perhaps washing their hands
or rubbing hand-hygiene gel over their hands,
along their fingers and across the webbing

between thumb and first finger, with which they point
to charts and scans and the overall direction,
which is towards their own death and your death,
the death of the planet and the death of hope

which of all things they aim to keep alive.
When you leave your white hospital bed to someone
with more need of their attention, hope will climb
up the steep side of the undersheet, lie back

relieved, against several pillows, and, docile, watch
the thermometer homing in on its open mouth.
Hope will be sitting cheerfully up in bed,
surrounded by cards and x-rays and relatives,

while you are wheeled along the corridors,
no longer in pain, a sheet over your face.

*Ruth Valentine*

# Legacy

My grandfather remembered the old ways,
talked about the poor house,
marvelled at the clean sheets, nurses.
*All this for free.*

At five, it felt I flew
from home to operating table.
Back in the garden, playing,
I couldn't understand my mother's tears.

Photos on my phone,
my tiny granddaughter, drip in arm.
Waiting, praying, knowing
*she's in good hands.*

Dear NHS,
I am mid-span
in five generations
that have known your care.

Without your saving skills in 1956,
ten of us would never have been here.

*Fiona Ritchie Walker*

# A Medical History

Yes, now I remember him,
though it was really his wife
who came in for his medicine
as he was too busy. It seemed
to work well for us all
as you can see on his card—
the repeats at regular intervals

*Male: Summary of Treatment Card*

Later she said he needed some help
with sleep, so we gave her
Temazepam for him—
another repeat. To make life simpler
it too went on the card.
Computers were coming
but not yet arrived

*This record is the property of the Family Health Services Authority*

It was she who was taking them
as is often the case—
we realised one day when
she cried at Reception—
I fitted her in. He was the problem.
Not eating I wrote in his notes
and said he should come in

*This column has been provided for Doctors to enter A, V or C at their discretion*

He was jaundiced already, but
we did the bloods which showed
obstruction. No pain. It was obvious
urgent referral was needed.
He was seen by the surgeons—
no treatment, ca pancreas
as we knew all along

*The Doctor should see that the particulars on the front are properly filled in*

She continued Temazepam
with district nurse daily
after I got them to set up
a driver. It worked well—
Diamorph and sedation of course
makes a good death. I think
she still takes them—I ought to check

*Cause of Death*
Doctor's signature and Date

Richard Westcott

# Guy's Hospital, October 2015

In the waiting room a game show called *The Edge*
combines bowling skills with general knowledge.
Nobody watches or changes the channel.
I carry a chewed polystyrene cup

to the ward that's wired with orange poison.
There's a woman who looks worse than you,
wearing a cold cap that fuses *Tron*
with 50s swimwear fashion. Her husband

loiters. I think *please never let this happen*
—I give you water—*to me*. Your fingernails
are gone. Outside the window, sunlight streams
through The Shard and London Bridge Station.

Natalie Whittaker

# Endoscopy

My doctor sent me
to have an endoscopy.

The instruments they used
made me gag and retch,

and in the end they said
they couldn't find anything wrong with me,

that the burning in my guts
was probably just love,

and there was nothing they could do
about that.

*Joe Williams*

# For Mary, Ward 26

You sit, frail as a grass stem
bent against yourself.
Leaning sideways, you look at tomorrow
which stands behind you,
a grey shape with no name.

I ask you to name the shape.
You give it words.
I hear your words, catch them
for a moment in the air.

I touch your arm.
You look away from the postcard
of striped deck chairs facing
an empty blue sea that I give to you.

'I don't know . . .' you say.

*Sue Wood*

# Notes and Acknowledgements

'Please Follow the Yellow Line' was first published in *Anatomy of a Whale* (Onslaught Press, 2018).

'Head to Head' is dedicated to Kate Swindlehurst. It was first published in *Poetry in Moments: Poems for a Hospital Community* by Jo Shapcott, Eve Lacey, Rebecca Watts & Kaddy Benyon, as part of the Taking Note project run by Cambridge Curiosity and Imagination and Addenbrooke's Arts.

'The Memory Clinic' was first published in *The Hippocrates Prize Anthology of Winning and Commended Poems 2017*, The Hippocrates Press, London (2017).

'On hearing for the first time' won third prize in the Hippocrates Prize for Poetry and Medicine and was published in the *Hippocrates Prize Anthology*.

'Changed' has, in an earlier form, been posted on Jo Bell's '52' Facebook page and previously appeared in the Easter Special Edition of a Good Dadhood https://gooddadhood.com/easter-special-edition/.

'Chopin in the ICU'—In 2011, I spent two days in the Neuro intensive care unit in Queen's Hospital, Romford following surgery to remove a spinal tumour. Despite being an emotional and traumatic experience, it has been hard for me to write much about it. But given the opportunity to write in celebration of the 70th anniversary of the NHS, it was the dedication and care I received from the medical staff that came back to inspire me, together with the strange trains of thought that come and go in a mind addled with painkilling drugs.

'Chemo Nurse' was first published In the *The Goldsmith's Apprentice*, published by Fair Acre Press, 2018.

'Keeping Borzoi' was highly commended in the Bare Fiction Prize for Poetry, 2016.

'In Patient' was included in the poetry wall at Addenbrookes hospital for Taking Note Cambridge Curiosity and Imagination 2017.

Thanks to the editors of *Blackbox Manifold*, who first published 'Scapegoats' under a different title in issue 19.

'Mothers' was written during a residency at the John Radcliffe Hospital, Oxford in the children's cancer ward. As an artist I was working with the children using poetry, painting and modelling. Their work was exhibited at the hospital at the end of the residency. I am very grateful to Anne Stevenson, who was part of the hospital school for setting up the residency and to all the staff who supported my work during the project.

'Mummy and the Night Sky' will be included in my debut pamphlet *The Dancing Boy*, which will be published by Against the Grain Press in 2019.

'Night Operations' was written for the St Magnus Festival Writers' Course in 2017, and was subsequently published online on the George Mackay Brown Fellowship website as part of Henge on the Surge. The poem describes an air ambulance flight from the Isle of Benbecula to Glasgow in late January 2003. My son had appendicitis, which I had mistaken for a tummy bug for a couple of days. A neighbour of mine, pregnant with her eldest, was also on the same flight and we both will always remember that night, and how well we were looked after.

'The Day You Took my Hand' was awarded second place in the 2018 RNIB writing competition and appears on the RNIB website.

'Hospital Coffee' was first published in *The Lightbulb has Stigmata* (Onslaught Press, 2016).

'Mrs Bate Addresses the College of Physicians, 1601' was previously published by The Littoral Press in Maggie Freeman's collection *Singing for Mr Bear* (2014).

'It's About a Man' won 1st prize in the Hippocrates Poetry Competition in 2010 and is included in *Born in the NHS* an anthology of poetry, anecdote and memoir about being brought up in doctors' households and working also in the NHS, co-written with Jane Kirwan and published by Hippocrates press 2013. Jane worked as a dentist and I worked with people suffering from mental health problems in hospitals and the community.

'Blood Letting' is from a long sequence called 'From Requiem for the Engineer', published in *Litmus* haematological issue (2015), *Of Heads & Hearts*, Shearsman Books (2018) and *The Forward Book of Poetry 2019*, (Bookmark, 2018).

'The opening lines of Heartbeat' contain a reference to Carol Ann Duffy's poem 'Mrs Midas' from *The World's Wife* (Picador 1999).

'Haiku' were previously published in *Haiku Journal*, *Presence Magazine*, Inner Voices International Womens' Haiku Festival (jenniferhambrick.com).

'Unexpected Benefits of Phototherapy' was written in response to (although not strictly about!) my experience of phototherapy to treat 'intransigent eczema'. It was originally published in *Domestic Cherry*, Issue 6.

'Coma' was published in *Child: New and Selected Poems 1991-2011* by Carcanet Press 2011.

'Psalm' was published in *Paraphernalia* (Bloodaxe Books, 2007).

'Student' was originally published in *The Sun Bathers* (Shoestring Press, 2013).

'The Surgery I Go to Has a Two-Headed Doctor (a.k.a. The government's latest cost-saving innovation for the NHS)' was previously published by Spilling Cocoa Over Martin Amis, under the title 'Doctor Smith'.

'Reflections of the Man in the Iron Mask' appeared in *The Year of the Crab*, in 2017 by Cultured Llama Publishing.

'I Remember L.A.2' was originally published in *Southend Poetry 98*.

'Orthopaedic Surgeon' was originally published in *Small Nuclear Family* (Eyewear, 2015).

'All These Things That I Have Done'—I would like to acknowledge my lovely friend Kjell who has been alongside me through every poem I've ever written. This poem and all poems are for my Mother Shelagh who passed away Dec 2016. Every word is for her.

'Radiography' was shortlisted in The Hippocrates Prize for Poetry & medicine. It was originally published in Angela Readman's collection *The Book of Tides* (Nine Arches, 2016).

'Crohn Heroine'—as spoken backdrop to Richard Crow and desperate optimists hospital video published in 'Essay on the Space Outside Pain where the Poem Takes Place' in E. Polledo-Gonzales and J.S. Tarr eds. *Painscapes: Communicating Pain*, (London: Palgrave-Macmillan, 2017).

'Birth Rite' was first published in *Changing the Subject* (Oxford University Press, 1990).

'Bath' was first published in *Multiplying the Moon* (Enitharmon Press, 2004).

'On the ceiling' was first published in *Will you walk a little faster?* (Bloodaxe, 2017).

'Love Song in a Bleached Room' was first published in *The Visitations* (Seren, 2013).

Poem for Badger—I thank the staff of Eastboune General Hospital for inspiring me to write the poem.

'The State Of The Asylum' was originally published in *New Boots and Pantisocracies*, ed. W N Herbert and Andy Jackson (https://newbootsand-pantisocracies.wordpress.com/).

'In the waiting room' has been published in *The Journal* poetry magazine, and in *ident* published by The Onslaught Press in 2017.

'Night Before an Operation' was first published in *The Fat Damsel* and was including in my Indigo Dreams collection *Rosary of Ghosts*.

'Ultrasound' came from my experience of antenatal ultrasound scans at my local hospital, Ealing for my three children, now all young adults. It addresses the mystery of seeing inside my own body and the anticipation of imagining what kinds of people these unknown babies will turn out to be. Luckily they're all making their own way in the world and all very different. I had excellent antenatal care but sadly Ealing Hospital's maternity unit has suffered under recent government cuts and now women have to travel out of the borough to give birth.

'Topical Iodine' first appeared in *A Bee's Breakfast* (Beautiful Dragons 2017). In the 1950s, a standard treatment for cuts and scrapes was an application of iodine tinted with gentian violet. The treatment is now obsolete.

'Long-term Prognosis' was first published in *Downpour* (Smokestack 2014).

'Legacy' won the Royal London Hospital's poetry competition, held as part of its NHS at 70 celebrations.

'A Medical History' —I wrote this many years ago as an NHS GP, before computerisation had arrived. It describes the use of, and reflects upon, the old written records we used to use—A6 size cards (various colours) that slotted into a special envelope—with narrow lines, headings and columns, encouraging very brief but succinct comments. So it's a sort of history in itself, using (and demonstrating) a now obsolete (but within living memory) recording system that influenced/coloured the care given, along with the language used, as well as the whole approach —so, a medical history, in two senses of the word.

'Guy's Hospital, October 2015' was first published in *Brittle Star* Issue 41, and later in the pamphlet *Shadow Dogs* (ignitionpress 2018).

'Endoscopy' originally appeared in Joe's pamphlet *Killing the Piano*, published by Half Moon Books, and was also included in *Sarasvati* Issue 50.

'For Mary, Ward 26' is from the NHS-supported writing project 'Acute Elderly', Leeds General Infirmary.

# Biographies

Matt Barnard is a poet and writer. His first full collection, *Anatomy of a Whale*, was published in 2018 by the Onslaught Press. He was born in London where he still lives with his wife, two sons and two dogs. He edits the blog www.britishlifeinpoetry.co.uk.

Becky Balfourth is a mental health worker and also a service user. She writes, runs & reads in her spare time and has a blog on self-harm and mental health issues.

Diana Bell is a multi-media artist using sculpture, installation, painting and public participation work. Her installations often link across art forms including poetry, dance and music. She has won several awards for her work including a Clore Duffield Award for her work in hospitals. www.dianabell.co.uk

Kaddy Benyon is a Granta New Poet. Her first collection, *Milk Fever* (Salt, 2012), won the Crashaw Prize. She is also the author of *The Tidal Wife* (Salt, 2018). A former television scriptwriter for Hollyoaks and Grange Hill, Kaddy was recently Invited Poet at The Polar Museum in Cambridge.

Roger Bloor is a retired NHS psychiatrist and is currently an MA student in Poetry Writing from Newcastle University studying at the London Poetry School. His poems have been published in anthologies including the *Hippocrates Prize Anthology* (2017) and also in *Still Born* (Affect Publications) and magazines including *Magma*.

Carole Bromley lives in York where she runs poetry surgeries for the Poetry Society and is the Stanza rep. She has three collections with Smith/Doorstop, *A Guided Tour of the Ice House*, *The Stonegate Devil* and *Blast Off!* (for children).

Sarah J Bryson is a poet, hospice nurse and keen photographer. Her poetry has been placed in competitions, published in anthologies, in journals and on line. She is interested in writing for well being, and has been involved in a Creative Ageing project, taking poetry into residential care.

Rachel Burns poetry has been published in literary magazines, recently in *The Fenland Reed*, *Head Stuff*, *South Bank Poetry*, *Marble Poetry* and *A Restricted View from Under the Hedge*.

David Canning's first collection, *An Essex Parish*, was published in 2015. He has been published in several anthologies and magazines, long-listed in the National Poetry Competition, shortlisted for the Bridport Prize and won first prize in the Sentinel Quarterly Review Competition. He performs around Essex and Suffolk and is on Essex Poetry Festival's organising committee.

Mark Cassidy is an NHS radiographer by trade, who reads now and again in Portsmouth and beyond. His poems—written in the gaps between work, home and birdwatching—have appeared in several magazines and anthologies. He'd like to see the world with x-ray vision.

Keith Chandler's poetry has been published in collections by Carcanet, OUP, Redbeck and Peterloo. His latest collection, *The Goldsmith's Apprentice*, published by Fair Acre Press in 2018, is the winner of The Rubery International Award for Poetry. Website: KeithChandlerPoet.com

Claire Collison is artist in residence at the Women's Art Library. Her poetry was placed in the Hippocrates Prize 2017 (2nd) and the inaugural Resurgence Prize for ecopoetry (2nd). Claire is currently developing her single-breasted life modelling monologue, *Truth is Beauty*, which she plans to tour. writingbloomsbury.wordpress.com

Clare Crossman lives outside Cambridge. She has published three collections of poetry with Shoestring Press. The Blue Hour is the most recent. In 2018 she also published Winter Flowers a short biography of the Cumbrian artist Lorna Graves. She is working on a fourth collection. She was seriously ill last year and the NHS did everything for her.

Claire Crowther's most recent collections are *On Narrowness* (Shearsman 2015) and *Bare George* (Shearsman, 2015). *Hap*, a short collection, is due from Happenstance in 2019.

Michelle Diaz has been published in several journals, both online and print e.g *Prole*, *Algebra of Owls*, *Picaroon*, *Atrium*, among others. She was recently awarded 1st prize in the Christabel Hopesmith NHS Competition. Her debut pamphlet *The Dancing Boy* is due out in 2019 with Against the Grain Press.

Geri Dogmetchi was born in London. She lived abroad until 1979 and after her return to the UK worked as a psychotherapist in the NHS. Still working in private practice, she has been writing poetry for some years. Her poem in this anthology was inspired by her work in the NHS and a broken leg.

Catherine Eunson (catherineeunson.net) and her family lived in the Outer Hebrides for twenty years, where she worked in music, the arts and education. Now living in Glasgow she particularly enjoys public transport and poetry meet ups in cafés. Catherine also wrote and recorded music for Pauline Prior-Pitt's *North Uist Sea Poems*.

Sarah Evans has had many short stories published in anthologies and magazines. Prizes have been awarded by: Words and Women, Winston Fletcher Prize, Stratford Literary Festival and Rubery. Other publishing outlets include: the Bridport Prize, Unthank Books, Riptide, Best New Writing and Shooter. Writing poetry is a more recent venture.

Helen Fletcher is the author of *the lightbulb has stigmata* published by the Onslaught Press. She is Catholic and studied English and German Literature before moving to Cumbria. She is working on her second collection and sends out thanks to the staff of the Special Care Baby Unit at Carlisle Infirmary after the birth of her twin daughters.

Maggie Freeman lives in East London. Some of her poems have been published in Acumen, Stand and The Rialto. Her three historical novels are being republished by Sapere Books. She also writes short stories.

Wendy French ran a school in a psychiatric hospital for many years and left early to develop writing workshops in healthcare communities. From 2014-15 I was Poet in Residence at the UCH Macmillan Centre London. *My Book Thinks Itself a Hawk*, pub: Hippocrates press, was a result of this residency.

Owen Gallagher was born of Irish parents in the Gorbals area of Glasgow. He now lives in London. Previous publications: *Sat Guru Snowman*, Peterloo Poets, 2001; *Tea with the Taliban*, Smokestack Books, 2012: *A Good Enough Love*, Salmon Poetry, Ireland, 2015, nominated for the T.S.Eliot award. *Clydebuilt* will be published by Smokestack Books in 2019.

Mark Gilbert writes short prose, poetry and non-poetry. His work is published in various international journals.

Lucy Hamilton co-edited *Long Poem Magazine* 2008-2018. Now an editor for Cam Rivers Publishing (UK/China), King's College, Cambridge. Collection *Stalker* (Shearsman, 2012) shortlisted for the Forward Prize for Best First Collection. *Of Heads & Hearts* (Shearsman, 2018). Combined artwork and poetry in *Long Exposure, Ink, Sweat & Tears, The Wolf* and *Molly Bloom*.

Alexander Hamilton is a Property Maker, Mixed Media Artist, and Accidental Farmer. Having spent his working life in the Theatre, words have been the background to his every day. When not at his bench, he writes short stories and poetry, some of which have been accepted for Forward Poetry anthologies.

A Doctor of anthropology, Jenny Hammond has written two books on Ethiopia and also collected their (mostly oral) poetry before turning to poetry writing herself about twelve years ago. It has been her delight ever since. She lives near Oxford.

John Hawkhead is a writer from the South West of England whose haiku have been published all over the world. He specializes in short-form writing from one-minute plays to one line poems compressing as much meaning as possible into very small spaces.

Beda Higgins is an award winning author and poet. She has two collections of short stories published: *Chameleon* and *Little Crackers*; and has poetry published in a wide range of anthologies. She lives in Newcastle upon Tyne.

Angi Holden is a retired Creative Writing lecturer whose poetry and short-fictions, widely published online and in print, explore family history and personal experience. Her pamphlet *Spools of Thread*, published in Spring 2018, won the inaugural Mother's Milk Pamphlet Prize.

Amanda Huggins is the author of the flash fiction collection, *Brightly Coloured Horses* (Chapeltown Books), and the short story collection, *Separated From the Sea* (Retreat West Books). She is also a published poet and award winning travel writer. She lives in Yorkshire and works in engineering.

Mimi Khalvati has published eight collections with Carcanet Press, including *The Meanest Flower*, shortlisted for the TS Eliot Prize, and *Child: New and Selected Poems*, a PBS Special Commendation. A new collection is forthcoming in 2019. She is a Fellow of the Royal Society of Literature.

Joanne Limburg is a writer and creative writing lecturer. Her most recent books are *The Autistic Alice* (Bloodaxe Books, 2017) and *Small Pieces* (Atlantic Books, 2017). Without the NHS, she would not be here.

Julie Lumsden is published in a Shoestring anthology called *Strike up the Band* (2017), *One for the Road* (smith/doorstop, 2017) and *poems for Grenfell Tower* (Onslaught, 2018). She lives in north Derbyshire with her husband.

Bernadette Lynch's poetry moves between England and Ireland as does she. Her poems have been published in anthologies in both countries including *Centenary in Reflection* 2016 and *Poems for Grenfell Tower* 2018. She writes about people, places and connections. She loves the energy created by reading her poetry to an audience.

Sue MacIntyre's working life has been as an editor in book publishing. Her debut collection, *The Wind Today*, was published by Hearing Eye in 2010 and she has also brought out two pamphlets—*Picnic with Seafog and Elephants* (The Many Press) and *Green City* (Stonewood Press, Thumbprint series).

Roy Marshall worked as a nurse in cardiology, coronary care and renal research. He currently works in adult education. His collection *The Sun Bathers* (2013) was nominated for the Michael Murphy award and his recent collection *The Great Animator* (Shoestring Press, 2017) includes 'Traces', a sequence about his nursing experiences.

Al McClimens is an unemployed waster. He reads fiction and writes poetry. He once came 134th in the National Poetry competition and nobody is allowed to forget this. He will work for food.

Thomas McColl lives in East London. His first full collection of poetry, *Being With Me Will Help You Learn*, was recently published by Listen Softly London Press, and he's been featured in various anthologies, including *Poems for Jeremy Corbyn* (Shoestring Press) and *Poems for Grenfell Tower* (The Onslaught Press).

Gill McEvoy: winner of the 2015 Michael Marks award for the pamphlet *The First Telling* (Happenstance Press, 2014). Two collections: *Rise* and *the Plucking Shed*, Cinnamon Press, 2013 and 2010. Awarded a Hawthornden Fellowship 2012.

Gordon Meade is a Scottish poet based in the East Neuk of Fife. He divides his time between his own writing and developing creative writing courses for vulnerable people in a variety of settings. His ninth collection, *The Year of the Crab*, was published in 2017 by Cultured Llama Publishing.

Gillian Mellor lives in Moffat, Scotland, helps to run The Moffat Bookshop. She co-authored the pamphlet *Compass Points* with three writing friends launched at Big Lit in Gatehouse-of-Fleet and won third prize in the 2018 Clochoderick Poetry Competition.

Joan Michelson's poetry books: *The Family Kitchen*, 2018, The Finishing Line Press, KY, *Landing Stage*, 2017, publication prize, SPM Publishers, UK, *Bloomvale Home*, 2016, Original Plus Chapbooks, Wales, 2016. *Toward The Heliopause*, 2011, and *Into the Light*, 2008, Poetic Matrix Press, CA. Originally from New England Joan lives in London, England.

Lucy Newlyn is Emeritus Fellow in English at St Edmund Hall Oxford where she taught for over thirty years. She has published widely on English Romanticism, and is the author of two collections of poetry: *Ginnel* (Cacanet, 2005) and *Earth's Almanac* (Enitharmon, 2015).

Colin Newton is active in an autism charity following early retirement on health grounds. His debut novella *The Atlas Legacy* explores a unique solution to an ancient mystery. Several of his poems are available online.

Kate Noakes' most recent collection is *Paris, Stage Left* (2017). Her new book, *The Filthy Quiet*, will be published by Parthian in 2019. Her website, boomslangpoetry.blogspot.com, is archived by the National Library of Wales. She lives in London and is a trustee of literature advocacy organisation, Spread the Word.

Nick Pallot is a pensioner who is increasingly surprised that the young aren't angrier at the state of the world being bequeathed to them. He has taken up poetry as a way of leaving something of his own feelings about it for his children.

Matthew Paul was born in 1966. His collection, *The Evening Entertainment* was published by Eyewear in 2017. He is also the author of two collections of haiku and co-writer/editor of *Wing Beats: British Birds in Haiku*, all published by Snapshot Press, and has contributed to the Guardian's 'Country Diary' column.

Mel Pryor's collection *Small Nuclear Family* (Eyewear 2015) was described by the TLS as "a remarkable debut" and was a *Daily Mail* Christmas poetry book of the year. She won the 2015 Philip Larkin Poetry Prize and in February 2018 was the Scottish Poetry Library digital poet-in-residence.

Anna Rankin was born and raised on the Wirral but is currently residing in Liverpool. At weekends you'll find her with her husband Jerry and their dog Watson hiking somewhere in the countryside. If its raining she'll be curled up with a book or film joined by her cats Poppy and Jasper.

Angela Readman's poems have won The Mslexia Poetry Competition, The Charles Causey and The Essex Poetry Prize. Her latest collection *The Book of Tides* was published by Nine Arches (2016). She also writes short stories.

Jude Rosen is an urban researcher, translator, poet. *A Small Gateway* was published by Hearing Eye, 2009. Her collection *Reclamations* is forthcoming. She collaborated with Richard Crow on a hospital video, and neuroscientists, clinical researchers and fellow sufferers of chronic pain on its artistic representation—*Painscapes: Communicating Pain* (Palgrave, 2017).

Carole Satyamurti is a poet and sociologist, who lives and works in London and for many years taught at the Tavistock Clinic. She won the National Poetry Competition in 1986, and a Cholmondeley Award in 2000. *Countdown* (Bloodaxe, 2011) is her first new collection since *Stitching the Dark: New & Selected Poems* (Bloodaxe, 2005).

Robert Schechter is a writer of children's poetry and adult light verse and translations. His poems have appeared widely in magazines and anthologies.

Myra Schneider's recent collections are *The Door to Colour* (Enitharmon 2014) and the pamphlet *Persephone in Finsbury Park*, (Second Light Publications (2016) Other publications include books about personal writing. She is consultant to the Second Light Network. Her new collection, 2018, is *Lifting the Sky* from Ward Wood Publishing.

Finola Scott is widely published including *The Ofi Press, Ink, Sweat & Tears, Firth*. A performance poet she enjoys reading especially in unusual places such as Rosslyn Chapel, by candlelight; EIBF; the Scottish Parliament. Finola enjoys Poetry Tourism, reading at far-flung launches, making new pals.

Penelope Shuttle has made her home in Cornwall since 1970 and the county's mercurial weather and rich history are continuing sources of inspiration. So too is the personal and artistic union Shuttle shared with her husband, the poet Peter Redgrove, until his untimely death in 2003. She has published many collections of poetry, the most recent being *Will you walk a little faster?* (Boodaxe, 2017).

Kathryn Simmonds has published two poetry collections with Seren Books, *Sunday at the Skin Launderette* (2008) and *The Visitations* (2013). She lives in Norwich with her family and is working on another book.

Reuben Roy Smith has scribbled many things during his life, both poems and short stories and has had bits and pieces published. He is a member of the famous Polari Literary group which puts on performances around the country and the Southbank Centre in London.

Ruth Steadman is a writer and CBT Therapist, and worked for the NHS for eleven years before moving into full-time private practice in 2017. Her poetry has been published in *Popshot Magazine, Ink Sweat and Tears, The High Window, New Boots and Pantisocracies, Disclaimer Magazine* and the Royal Academy's blog.

Hannah Stone has two collections of poetry, *Lodestone* (2016) and *Missing Miles* (2017). She hosts the poets/composers forum for the Leeds Lieder Festival. The premiere of her 'Penthos Requiem' forms part of the city's commemoration for the centenary of the end of the Great War. Her older son is a junior doctor.

Alan John Stubbs was born in Salford and now lives in Cumbria. He is a prize winner in the Arvon International Poetry Competition 2008, and has been shortlisted in the Bridport Prize. The Onstaught Press has published his collections *ident* and *The Lost Box of Eyes*.

Grant Tarbard is the co-founder of Resurgant Press & editorial assistant for Three Drops From A Cauldron. He is the author of *Loneliness is the Machine that Drives the World* (Platypus Press) and *Rosary of Ghosts* (Indigo Dreams).

Ali Thurm's poems have been published in magazines and anthologies. In 2017 she was a runner-up in the Troubadour International Poetry Prize, longlisted for the Bath Novel Award and shortlisted for the First Novel Award (Daniel Goldsmiths). She reviews poetry and fiction for The London Magazine and on her blog: https://alithurm.org

Angela Topping is the author of eight full poetry collections, four pamphlets and three critical books. She has benefited from the NHS all her life, being born in 1954 into a working class family. She blogs at angelatopping.wordpress.com. Poems have appeared in many journals and anthologies.

Ruth Valentine has published nine collections of poetry, as well as a novel and works of non-fiction. She lives in Tottenham, North London.

Susannah Violette lives in the endless forests of Germany with her husband and two daughters. Nature is the blood of her work. The animals both within us and outside of us fascinate her and her poems become liminal spaces where the edges of these worlds blur.

Fiona Ritchie Walker writes poetry and short fiction. She was a full-time carer for her husband until he died in 2016. She won Carers UK's 2015 creative writing competition and her poetry sequence, *After Diagnosis,* is published by Hybrid Press's House of Three.

After a professional lifetime as an NHS GP in a small market town, Richard Westcott now has the time to concentrate on his writing, which has won various prizes and commendations. Details of his well-received first poetry book may be found at www.indigodreams.co.uk/richard-westcott/4594230918 And he blogs at www.richardwestcottspoetry.com.

Natalie Whittaker's debut pamphlet, *Shadow Dogs* is published by ignitionpress. Natalie is a poet and secondary school teacher who lives in South East London.

Joe Williams is a writer and performing poet from Leeds. In 2017 his debut pamphlet, *Killing the Piano*, was published by Half Moon Books, and he won the prestigious Open Mic Competition at Ilkley Literature Festival. His second book, *An Otley Run*, will be published in December 2018. www.joewilliams.co.uk.

Sue Wood won 1st prize in the Oxford Literary Festival, was a winner in the Poetry Business Book and Pamphlet Competition, and came second in the Basil Bunting  Poetry Competition, Cinnamon Press Award for Poetry in 2008 leading to the publication of her first poetry collection *Imagine yourself to be water* (2010).

# Other Onslaught poetry titles

*Tomorrow is the Tugboat of Topday* (2018) Alan John Stubbs

*Glengower* (2018) Gabriel Rosenstock

*Poems for Grenfell Tower* (2018) ed. Rip Bulkeley

*Anatomy of a Whale* (2018) Matt Barnard

*Mandible* (2018) Ingrid Casey

*Flower Press* (2018) Alice Kinsella

*Long Days of Rain* (2017) Janak Sapkota

*Orpheus in the Underpass* (2017) Ross McKessock Gordon & Gabriel Rosenstock

*ident* (2016) Alan John Stubbs

*the lightbulb has stigmata* (2016) Helen Fletcher

*Out of the Wilderness* (2016) by Cathal Ó Searcaigh
with an introduction and translations by Gabriel Rosenstock

*You Found a Beating Heart* (2016) Nisha Bhakoo

*I Wanna Make Jazz to You* (2016) Moe Seager

*Tea wi the Abbot* (2016) Scots haiku by John McDonald
with transcreations in Irish by Gabriel Rosenstock

*Judgement Day* (2016) Gabriel Rosenstock

*We Want Everything* (2016) Moe Seager

*to kingdom come* (2016) ed. Rethabile Masilo

*The Lost Box of Eyes* (2016) Alan John Stubbs

*Antlered Stag of Dawn* (2015) Gabriel Rosenstock,
with translations by Mariko Sumikura & John McDonald

*behind the yew hedge* (2015) Mathew Staunton & Gabriel Rosenstock

*Bumper Cars* (2015) Athol Williams

*Waslap* (2015) Rethabile Masilo

*Aistear Anama* (2014) Tadhg Ó Caoinleáin

*for the children of Gaza* (2014) Mathew Staunton & Rethabile Masilo (eds.)